IMPRESSUM:

Max Teske
Alter Weg 10
38124 Braunschweig

Printed by Amazon Italia Logistica S.r.l.
Torrazza Piemonte (TO), Italy

51148164R00063